Mercy for Judas

Grasping the Depth of Christ's Love

Robert E. Colwell

Mercy for Judas
Grasping the Depth of Christ's Love
Robert E. Colwell © 2021

Contact Author at: www.mercyforjudas.com

ISBN 978-0-9988055-1-1

Cover design, layout, and artwork by:
Ashley Sasson

Published by:
Latte Media Group
1030 E. Hwy 377 Suite 110 Box 184
Granbury, TX 76048
www.Latte.Media

Neither the publisher nor the author is engaged in rendering professional advice or service to the individual reader. The ideas, suggestions, and procedures contained in this book are not intended as a substituted for consulting with your own personal professional support system.

All Scripture references are from the NKJV of the Holy Bible, unless otherwise noted. **All bolded Scripture references are the emphasis of the author.**

Contents

Introduction

FOLLOWERS OF JESUS CHRIST TODAY MAY FIND IT
DIFFICULT TO FATHOM THE RELATIONSHIP THAT GOD
ENJOYED WITH THE FIRST COUPLE, PRIOR TO THEIR
BETRAYAL. Though God's love never changed, betrayal
cost them the joy of walking with God in innocence. The
penalty for their sin was paid by God's Son, who sacrificed
His life that all might experience the joy of forgiveness and
the peace of being innocent in His presence. Therefore,
the Old Testament's teachings and the gospels in the New
Testament are accounts of God's providence in making
forgiveness of sins and reconciliation with God available
to all humankind.

Forgiveness of sins is possible only because of God's
mercy.

"For I will be merciful to their unrighteousness, and their sins and their lawless deeds I will remember no more."

(Hebrews 8:12)

Forgiveness of sins is something that an individual must want to experience. God extends forgiveness to all who earnestly seek it and teaches us through His Word to extend the same forgiveness to others. The need for forgiveness surfaces in all relationships but most notably in marriages. Love can't thrive in unforgiveness! Most people would likely agree that one of the most hurtful and difficult sins to forgive is betrayal. It *ruins, destroys, separates,* and makes *waste.* Waste is something that most conscientious people find disturbing, especially if what's being wasted is deemed to have value.

In John 12:3-6, Judas Iscariot expressed his resentment in seeing expensive oil wasted when it was poured out on Jesus' feet:

"Then Mary took a pound of very costly oil of

spikenard, anointed the feet of Jesus, and wiped His feet with her hair. And the house was filled with the fragrance of oil. But one of His disciples, Judas Iscariot, Simon's son, who would betray Him, said, **'Why was this fragrant oil not sold for three hundred denarii and given to the poor?'** *This he said, not that he cared for the poor but because* **he was a thief, and had the money box; and he used to take what was put in it.'"**

This waste of oil may have angered Judas; angry people sometimes do regrettable things, usually involving others and often without mercy. The point at which Judas began stealing from the money box and his reason for doing so is unknown. However, it appears that either anger or flawed reasoning is what motivated Judas to betray Jesus for thirty pieces of silver.

So, the question is, after experiencing the ultimate betrayal which led to His persecution and death, was there change in Jesus' attitude toward Judas? If yes, how so? Was He angry? How angry? On a scale of 1-10, with ten being greatest, what level do you think Jesus' anger reached? If He was not angry, did He pray for Judas or did He simply erase him from His mind?

Several Bible passages indicate that Jesus could perceive what was on the inside of man and knew in advance what men would do.

"But Jesus did not commit Himself to them, because He knew all men, and had no need that anyone should testify of man, for He knew what was in man."

(John 2:24-25)

Reflecting on the passage above, do you think Jesus was unaware of Judas' propensity to steal when He put him in charge of the moneybag? Knowing that Judas would betray Him, doesn't Jesus' selection of Judas for treasurer instead of Matthew, whose craft it was to handle money, seem strategic? And knowing that Judas was coming with soldiers to betray Him, did Jesus not purposely wait for them to arrive? Still the most important question for consideration is this: Did Jesus expect the betrayal to result in Judas being eternally separated from God?

If your answer to this last question is yes, are we to believe that the Messiah chose Judas as His disciple, knowing exactly what was in him; and then placed Judas in charge of the moneybox to allow his nature to unfold; and then permitted the dooming of Judas' soul for doing exactly what he was positioned to do? Are we to believe that the Messiah, the very personification of mercy, who came to earth to save the lost, would fulfill such a role for all of humankind *except for* Judas?

Furthermore, did Jesus anticipate that Judas would become remorseful? Did He not foresee that Judas would return the 30 pieces of silver and declare that he had sinned by betraying innocent blood? *(Matthew 27:3-5)*

Although our instinct is to hide or deny the sins we've committed, doing so prevents us from being real in our relationship with God. If sin is what separates us from God, then confessing our sin, as stated in Proverbs 28:13, is the path to receiving God's mercy: *"He who covers his sins will not prosper, but whoever confesses and forsakes them will have mercy."*

Reflecting on the above, is there mercy for Judas? Considering the person that Judas sinned against, most people would instinctively say, "No." Their answer is based on the belief that eternal damnation is an appropriate punishment for wasting the unspeakably valuable life of Jesus Christ. This presumed unforgivable evil offense and anger prevents many people from grasping the *loving merciful* nature that characterizes Christ.

The resolve of those who see no mercy for Judas is derived primarily from an interpretation of the words "lost" and "perdition" in John 17:12; which is contestable given the historical and literary context in which these words are used.

The following pronouncement from Mark 14:21, regarding the betrayer's fate, lends also to the traditional interpretation that Judas was beyond redemption:

"Woe to that man by whom the Son of Man is betrayed! It would have been good for that man

if he had never been born."

At first glance, the above might lead readers to assume that an act of betrayal against the Son of Man would certainly warrant eternal separation from God. However, a close examination of the mercy, mission, and character of Christ, invites a compelling argument for the possibility, even the probability, that Jesus did forgive His guilt-ridden friend, who apparently was unable to forgive himself. Suicide is the murder of oneself. If God would forgive someone for murdering another human being, why would He not have mercy on a person who, being overwhelmed by the weight of his situation, resorted to taking his own life?

Admittedly, there's little scriptural evidence to directly support or deny the traditional conclusions about Judas' spiritual fate; not much is known about him beyond his betrayal. Yet, the boundless love, divine character, and sovereign will of God that's displayed throughout the Bible suggest that mercy for Judas is precisely what God intended.

The purpose of this book is to uncover the power of mercy, especially in the context of marriage, by carefully examining the depth of Christ's love, highlighting the thoughts and ways of God as set forth in Scripture, and by inspiring a commitment to seek truth over tradition. The goal is to reveal mercy, the misery-removing power of God, as something attainable for all, even for someone like Judas.

Introduction

Mercy
for
Judas

Grasping the Depth of Christ's Love

Robert E. Colwell

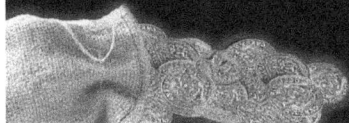

*Holiness, mercy, and love are the height
of God's character*

Mercy Precedes Everything

1

IT'S INTERESTING THAT SO MANY FOLLOWERS OF JESUS HOLD AN UNCEASING ANIMOSITY FOR JUDAS ISCARIOT. Other than Satan, Judas is arguably the most infamous figure in the Bible. Yet, his name is seldom mentioned in Christian circles until the subject of betrayal comes up. Yes, Judas betrayed the Messiah; and according to John's gospel, he stole from the money collected to support the ministry. However, the focal point in the betrayal narrative is the character of Jesus Christ. Similarly, in the story of the prodigal son, the point of the message isn't the foolishness of the son, but rather, the love of the father.

Why do so many believers maintain that mercy for Judas is out of the question? Regardless of one's education, church affiliation or length of time in the ministry, most people view Judas as *ineligible for mercy* without making any effort to determine why. In fact, it's hard, to date, to find anyone who would pose the notion that mercy for Judas could've been possible.

The weight of this issue cannot be overstated, for the consequences of believing that there is *no mercy for Judas* have been far-reaching and ruinous. Much of the anger, unforgiveness, violence, divorce, racism, and hatred throughout the civilized world can be traced to the belief that Jesus viewed Judas' sins as unpardonable. Even the slightest perception of flaw in Jesus' character might easily serve as license for the evil mentioned above. To misrepresent the impeccable character of Jesus Christ is, among other things, to distort His gospel message which calls for love, mercy, and forgiveness.

"Take heed to yourselves. If your brother sins against you, rebuke him; and if he repents, forgive

him. And if he sins against you seven times in a day, and seven times in a day returns to you, saying, 'I repent,' you shall forgive him."

(Luke 17:3-4)

"But if you do not forgive, neither will your Father in heaven forgive your trespasses."

(Mark 11:26)

"And forgive us our debts as we forgive our debtors...."

(Matthew 6:12)

The Bible is the most impactful book that the world has ever known. Its lessons regarding the proper consideration and treatment of others reverberate throughout both the faith and the secular communities. Therefore, to assert that Jesus showed no mercy for Judas affects relationships both human-to-human and human-to-divine, by inadvertently sanctioning unforgiveness.

If we could know assuredly that Jesus extended mercy to Judas and therefore could anticipate Judas joining in the heavenly chorus, it would yield a paradigm shift that would strip away the liberty to justify unforgiveness and restrain the rage to punish. Such knowledge would prompt us to balance God's Word against our own wrongdoings before criticizing or damning others. This might especially benefit couples, where instances of failing to forgive or show mercy can seem endless. Christ intended our acts of forgiveness to mimic His own.

*"Therefore, as the elect of God, holy and beloved, put on tender **mercies**, kindness, humility, meekness, longsuffering; bearing with one another, and **forgiving one another**, if anyone has a complaint against another; **even as Christ forgave you, so you also must do.**"*

(Colossians 3:12-13)

"And be kind to one another, tenderhearted, forgiving one another, even as God in Christ forgave you."

(Ephesians 4:32)

"And forgive us our debts as we forgive our debtors."

If we hold the belief that Judas died without any hope of forgiveness, do we not run counter to the mission and message of salvation? Is this what God intended Judas' narrative to convey—that stealing money and betraying a friend will result in **eternal separation from God?** Many interpret the bolded words below to mean, that the one who betrays the Son of Man will experience a fate worse than death—eternal damnation.

> *"The Son of Man indeed goes just as it is written of Him, but woe to that man by whom the Son of man is betrayed!* ***It would have been good for that man if he had not been born."*** *Then Judas, who was betraying Him, answered and said, 'Rabbi, is it I?' He said to him, 'You have said it.'"*
> *(Matthew 26:24-25)*

Though it's easy to construe Jesus' words as pertaining to spiritual doom, the subject of hell is not on the table. We should ponder what we already know about Christ's character and then ask ourselves, "Which makes better sense, that the *'woe'* statement in the above verse refers to life *after death* or rather, an unbearable suffering *here on earth* for the person who commits this evil betrayal?"

In John 17:12, Jesus prayed:

"While I was with them in the world, I kept them in Your name. Those whom you gave Me I have kept; and none of them is **lost** *except the son of perdition, that the Scripture might be fulfilled."*

While some might assume that the word "lost" in the above verse speaks of an ill-fated eternity, an alternative view is that by betraying Jesus, Judas *lost his office* of apostle and the privilege of being among the twelve who would *"go into all the world and preach the gospel...."* *(Mark 16:15).* In addition, by committing suicide, Judas *lost his place* among the living and went miserably to his grave—the place of his choosing. Acts 1:25 states: *"... that he might go to his own place."*

Some scholars believe that the above verse affirms that Judas was bound for hell, claiming that *"his own place"* means the place reserved exclusively for the wicked. This, according to them, is what Judas' evil mind preferred. However, "grave" and "hell" are not synonymous terms. The former suggests physical death, the latter speaks of spiritual death. It's senseless to think that Judas would choose the latter.

After subjecting his close Friend and Master to the traumatizing "power of darkness," it appears that Judas' haunting guilt was too overwhelming for him. Where and to whom could he turn? Imagine the reception he would've gotten had he sought consolation among the distraught disciples who were not yet filled with the Holy Spirit. Most likely Judas snapped under the weighty assumption that his pain would never go away. Therefore, in that dark moment, suicide seemed to be a better solution.

Some would argue that by taking his own life, Judas committed an unpardonable sin that would automatically make hell his eternal home. But let's consider Judas' sin alongside that of King David, who after killing Uriah and taking his wife Bathsheba for himself, appealed to God

Isn't restoration our Lord's desire for His followers who fall or turn away from the Truth?

for mercy:

> *"Have **mercy** upon me, O God, According to Your lovingkindness; According to the multitude of Your tender **mercies**, Blot out my transgressions. Wash me thoroughly from my iniquity, And cleanse me from my sin, For I acknowledge my transgressions, And my sin is always before me. Against You, You only, have I sinned, And done this evil in Your sight..."*
>
> *(Psalms 51:1-4)*

> *"For You do not desire sacrifice, or else I would give it; You do not delight in burnt offering. The sacrifices of God are a broken spirit, A broken and contrite heart—These, O God, You will not despise."*
>
> *(Psalms 51:16-17)*

If God would forgive the merciless crime of taking a man's life only to cover up for having slept with his wife, why would He not forgive the broken and contrite heart of Judas for taking his own life?

Holiness, mercy, and love are the height of God's character. Therefore, to say that Judas was ineligible for mercy, even though he remorsefully confessed his sin, would suggest that feelings and emotions factor into God's decision to extend mercy. Yet, there's no indication of that in Scripture nor is it consistent with Christ's character.

> *"And behold, a woman of Canaan came from that region and cried out to Him, saying, 'Have **mercy** on me, O Lord, Son of David! My daughter is severely demon-possessed.' But He answered her not a word. And His disciples came and urged Him, saying, 'send her away, for she cries out after us.'*
>
> *But He answered and said, 'I was not sent except to the lost sheep of the house of Israel.'*
>
> *Then she came and worshiped Him, saying, 'Lord, help me!'*
>
> *But He answered and said, 'It is not good to take the children's bread and throw it to the little dogs'*
>
> *And she said, 'Yes, Lord, yet even the little dogs eat the crumbs which fall from their masters'*

table.'

Then Jesus answered and said to her, 'O woman, great is your faith! Let it be to you as you desire.' And her daughter was healed from that very hour."

(Matthew 15:22-28)

"And behold, two blind men sitting by the road, when they heard that Jesus was passing by, cried out, saying, 'Have **mercy** on us, O Lord, Son of David!' Then the multitude warned them that they should be quiet; but they cried out all the more, saying, 'Have **mercy** on us, O lord, Son of David!' So Jesus stood still and called them, and said, 'What do you want Me to do for you?' They said to Him, 'Lord, that our eyes may be opened.' So Jesus had compassion and touched their eyes. And immediately their eyes received sight, and they followed Him.'"

(Matthew 20:30-34)

Similarly, in Luke 17:13, Jesus healed the 10 lepers:

"And they lifted up their voices and said, 'Jesus,

Master, have **mercy** on us!'" So when He saw
them, He said to them, 'Go show yourselves to
the priest.'" And so it was that as they went, they
were cleansed."

So, what is it, specifically, that rendered Judas
unfit for mercy? To say that Judas was an evil-hearted
person who disguised his true nature and never truly
repented for his betrayal is purely conjecture. An evil
thief wouldn't return to the temple to confess his sins
unless he was divinely inspired to do so. Throwing the
silver to the ground expresses emotions, feelings, and
an attitude that's inconsistent with that of a person who
was not genuinely sorry for having sinned.

Many believers contend that Judas never repented for
his sin. This Greek word (*metamelomai*) means to have
regret about something, in the sense that one wishes it
could be undone. It means to be very sorry. *Metamelomai*
is a synonym for the word (*metanoeo*), which means to
repent in several different contexts. It refers to changing
one's mind, repenting for sins practiced. The word most
often used for repentance from sin or evil is *metanoia*.

The issue with Judas wasn't *sinfulness* but rather the one-time *sin of betrayal*. A wrong view of a crime will result in inappropriate charges.

What if Jesus had been present to witness Judas' confession of sin and the throwing down of the 30 pieces of silver. Do you think Jesus' response would've been: "Sorry, Judas, I can't forgive you because you didn't specify the words, 'I repent?'" The Greek word (*metamelomai*) used in Matthew 27:3 is translated in the NKJV version as *remorse*. Though many popular Bibles use "remorse" in the above passage, there are at least nine other Bibles that translate this word as *repent*.

Is it reasonable that one would have deep sorrow over something he or she had done to another and not desire forgiveness? If Judas really wasn't an evil person but only acted foolishly, wouldn't the same inspiration that compelled him to confess his sin have led him to pray for forgiveness?

Some commentators use Jesus' words in the following verse to question whether Judas was ever a true believer.

*"Did I not choose you, the twelve, and **one of you is a devil?**" He spoke of Judas Iscariot, the son of Simon...."*

(John 6:70-71)

The above designation of "devil" wasn't used literally of Judas, any more than the word "Satan" was used literally in the following verse regarding Peter:

*"...He rebuked Peter, saying, 'Get behind Me, **Satan**! For you are not mindful of the things of God, but the things of men.'"*

(Mark 8:33)

If Judas wasn't a true believer, then he was one of the world's greatest actors, able to convince 11 fellow disciples, perhaps up to 12 hours a day for 3 years, that there was nothing questionable about his character. Even as Jesus spoke of His betrayer, while seated with the disciples at the Last Supper, they all asked the question *"Lord, is it I?"* None of them pointed to Judas or had a clue as to who the betrayer might be (Matthew 26:20-22). In every mention of Judas in the gospels there's nothing to suggest that Jesus or His disciples viewed Judas as being wicked. In fact, the apostle John's accounting of the above occurrence describes the disciples as being perplexed about who the betrayer might be.

> *"When Jesus had said these things, He was troubled in spirit, and testified and said, 'Most assuredly, I say to you, 'one of you will betray Me.' Then the disciples looked at one another **perplexed** about whom He spoke."*
>
> *(John 13:22)*

The fact that John's gospel refers to Judas as a thief and the betrayer of Christ, and that Jesus called Judas a *devil,* is insufficient justification for questioning the authenticity of Judas' conversion. How many of us behaved badly, *like a devil,* both before and after being converted to Christ? Matthew the former tax collector was a thief prior to his conversion. Yet, Jesus reached out to Matthew who later authored one of the four Gospels.

Although nothing is known of the betrayer apart from

his discipleship, there's no reason to think that Jesus was unaware of Judas' ambitious nature. Did Jesus not know that Judas could put his own personal well-being ahead of the mission, or that Judas would soon become the catalyst for ushering Him to the Cross? **And after doing exactly what Jesus expected Judas to do**, are we to believe that the Redeemer and Savior of the world, who preached about leaving the 99 to find the one that was lost, made no effort to preserve Judas' wayward soul? Isn't this inconsistent with what the Bible teaches about the mercy and love of Christ Jesus?

> *"What man of you, having a hundred sheep, if he loses one of them, does not leave the ninety-nine in the wilderness, and go after the one which is lost until he finds it? And when he has found it, he lays it on his shoulders, rejoicing. And when he comes home, he calls together his friends and neighbors, saying to them, Rejoice with me, for I have found my sheep which was lost! I say to you that likewise there will be more joy in heaven over one sinner who repents than over ninety-nine just persons who need no repentance."*

(Luke 15:4-7)

Isn't restoration our Lord's desire for all of His followers who fall or turn away from the Truth? Are there any examples in the gospels where the Lord *purposed* to banish a soul to destruction after the person acknowledged Christ's Lordship and followed Him?

> *Is it reasonable to think that Judas, having full knowledge of the depth of Christ's love, would return the money and hang himself without ever uttering the words, "Lord forgive me?"*

"I have manifested Your name to the men whom You have given Me out of the world…. For I have given to them the words which you have given Me; and they have received them, and have known surely that I came forth from You; and they have believed that You sent Me."

(John 17:6, 8)

Mercy is incompatible with selfishness

"All that the Father gives Me will come to Me, and the one who comes to Me I will by no means cast out. For I have come down from heaven, not to do My own will, but the will of Him who sent Me. This is the will of the Father who sent Me, that of all He has given Me I should lose nothing, but should raise it up at the last day. And this is the will of Him who sent Me, that everyone who sees the Son and believes in Him may have everlasting life; and I will raise him up at the last day."

(John 6:37-40)

"If we confess our sins, He is faithful and just to forgive us our sins and to cleanse us from all unrighteousness."

(I John 1:9)

Even more important than what Jesus wants us to understand about Judas, is what He wants us to believe and promote about Himself. Jesus is the personification of mercy and love. God's followers are instructed to learn of Christ's character and endeavor to become like Him:

*"Love has been perfected among us in this: that we may have boldness in the day of judgment; because **as He is, so are we in this world."***

19

(I John 4:17)

"For it is the God who commanded light to shine out of darkness, who has shone in our hearts to give the light of the knowledge of the glory of God in the face of Jesus Christ."

(II Corinthians 4:6)

The power to understand and faithfully express God's love is derived from the indwelling Holy Spirit. Yet, we won't sufficiently comprehend the depth of God's love until we've shared His love with others:

*"Love suffers long and is kind; love does not envy; love does not parade itself, is not puffed up; does not behave rudely, does not seek its own, is not provoked, **thinks no evil**; does not rejoice in iniquity, but rejoices in the truth; bears all things, believes all things, hopes all things, endures all things. Love never fails...."*

(I Corinthians 13:5)

"Beloved, let us love one another, for love is of God; and everyone who loves is born of God and

knows God. He who does not love does not know
God, for God is love."

(I John 4:7-8)

Knowledge of the depth of God's love is not casually acquired, it does not drift into our grasp. Therefore, the question of whether mercy was extended to Judas must be answered by viewing key biblical texts through the lens of God's love. Viewing people in the light of God's love helps us to better determine how and when to be merciful to others. Failure to show mercy is a betrayal of the Christian's calling and serves to legitimize unmercifulness in the eyes of those with a bent toward selfishness.

Selfishness was no doubt the root cause of Judas betraying the Messiah, as is true of most betrayals. Betrayal, in any form, is a terrible thing; pain, misery, and sufferings are always associated with it. Stealing is obviously a sin and a crime but who among us is guiltless? What then should we conclude about Judas' sin? Is it specifically the fact that he betrayed the holy "King of Kings" that makes his sin deserving of eternal damnation? Romans 2:11 tells us: *"For there is no partiality with God."*

God's response to a contrite heart's request for mercy is the same whether for stealing money or betrayal.

Selfishness is the soul of betrayal and manifests itself in all types of relationships. *Betrayal* is defined as: *To break faith with; fail to meet the hopes of; to lead astray; deceive; to seduce and then desert; to reveal unknowingly or against one's wishes.*[1] The devastation of betrayal is displayed more prominently in marriages. Therefore, showing mercy to our mate and to others, especially when they've sought it, helps to prove that we belong to God and that we delight to walk before Him in obedience. God's promise in Matthew 5:7 is that our acts of mercy will result in mercy being returned to us.

"Blessed are the merciful, for they shall obtain mercy."

Mercy is incompatible with selfishness. Mercy compels us to consider what another person is experiencing and the effect that our actions may have on them before we act. Always, God's followers are required to show mercy.

"Therefore, as the elect of God, put on tender mercies; kindness, humility, meekness, long-suffering; bearing with one another, and forgiving one another, if anyone has a complaint against another; even as Christ forgave you, so you also must do."

(Colossians 3:12-13)

"Therefore be merciful even as your Father is merciful."

(Luke 6:36)

In Luke 10:25-37, Jesus told a certain lawyer about a Samaritan traveler who stopped and cared for a man who'd been wounded by thieves, stripped of his clothing, and left for dead. In the story, a priest and a Levite had previously passed by the man but didn't stop to offer aid. Jesus then asked the lawyer:

*"So which of these three do you think was neighbor to him who fell among the thieves?" And he said, 'He who showed **mercy** on him.' Then Jesus said to him, **'Go and do likewise.'"***

23

Words delivered kindly in love promote healing, peace, and hope. . .

2

FEW THINGS ARE MORE TRAUMATIZING THAN HAVING A MARRIAGE DEVASTATED BY BETRAYAL. It's therefore imperative now, in these times of great discouragement and deception, that every effort be made to determine, during *courtship*, if *Sweetheart* has the propensity to betray.

Courtship is an exciting time of truth-seeking and trust-building, in the hope that a bright future together might be possible. If you build your mate's hopes during courtship that certain things will occur but apply no effort toward its actualization once married, that's betrayal.

The unreasonable, unexpected change from the position that you held during courtship, without explanation, is betrayal. To communicate continually during courtship but resort to one-sentence responses once married is again betrayal. Also, having no remorse for the waste that you caused or could've easily prevented, is a form of betrayal, and the list goes on. Courtship is meant to be a heartfelt, subtle but prudent investigation of one's character. Therefore, an insufficient courtship is self-betrayal.

No matter how honorable our intentions in courtship or how sincerely we regard our marriage vows, none of us can guarantee that we'll do only those things that'll make our spouse happy once married. Happiness is fleeting; today you have it, tomorrow you don't, the next day you have it again. Logical people understand this and therefore, happiness doesn't usually top their list of imperatives for marriage. Even though happiness is a priority, unhappiness is seldom the root cause of betrayal. Betrayal, for the most part, is sourced in feelings of inadequacy. These feelings may have little or nothing to do with one's spouse, although these feelings may be exacerbated by that spouse.

Most of us, at some point, have had feelings of inadequacy. Fewer of us have had caring capable people to help us overcome those feelings. One sure way to help build your mate's confidence is by daily exhibiting a life of fidelity.

Fidelity is faithful devotion to duty, obligation, or vows.[2] It springs from integrity and is marked by consistency. It resists negative outside influences, as well as selfish inner compulsions. Fidelity is evidenced by a continuous and proper response to that inner voice which helps us to recall things like: *You promised! You know better than that! That's illegal! You're married!* Furthermore, it asks questions like: Is she or he comfortable with this? *Is this your best? Is this what they or Scripture had in mind? Should you be looking at that?*

Fidelity is all about controlling imaginations. Humankind has been marvelously equipped to look at complicated situations and imagine the desired outcome and the steps necessary to make it reality. Without such ability it would be impossible to navigate this complex violent world.

Often, with many strained marriages, the issue isn't that the marriage can't be fixed or that the parties don't want it fixed, but rather, one or both spouses refuse to do what "fixing it" requires. Each believing themself to be the victim, insisting that the other must change. Instead of wasting time nursing thoughts of evil, retaliation, rebellion, or violence, they should ponder together the depth of Christ's love that's found in Judas' story, and embrace the difficult truth that, even in betrayal, love is called upon to *think no evil.* Love believes that the Holy Spirit will make the way of escape *(I Corinthians 10:13)*; therefore, love *"bears all things, believes all things, hopes all things, endures all things." (I Corinthians 13:7)*

Perfection is typically not the basis on which one chooses a mate, but rather, the person's capacity to fulfill certain needs or help in achieving specific goals. This was modeled by Jesus in His choice of twelve companions who were far from perfect but well-suited to make His mission successful. Yet, unlike Jesus who could readily forgive Judas because He knew the true state of his heart, we don't always know what lurks within our mate's heart, or even our own. Therefore, in rough times, communications with our spouse must be inspired by God's Word and guided by the Holy Spirit.

Words delivered kindly in love promote healing, peace, and hope; while the same message delivered with cruel intent, a frowned face, and angry tone, serve to water the seeds of destruction. We must pray, preferably together, for the grace to stay humble and to maintain fidelity, both to our marriage and to God's Word, and then trust that when problems arise, the marriage won't be jeopardized.

If mercy precedes everything we say and do, God's love won't permit us to pursue evil or think evil of our marriage or our mate.

When we betray our godly character by refusing to be merciful, we're not much different than Judas

3

AS STATED IN THE INTRODUCTION, ANGRY PEOPLE
SOMETIMES DO REGRETTABLE THINGS, USUALLY
INVOLVING OTHERS AND TYPICALLY WITHOUT
MERCY. Perhaps witnessing the costly oil being poured
out on Jesus' body and hearing him speak of His death
and burial *(Matthew 26:12)*, incited Judas to run to the
chief priest and ask, *"What are you willing to give if I
deliver Him to you?" (Matthew 26:15)*

Here's where we begin to look closely at Judas and ask
ourselves, "Why, despite all that we know about God's
Word and Christ's character, are we quick to embrace

commonly held negative conclusions concerning Judas?" Why are we so casual in our consideration of him? Could selfishness, which serves as an impediment to godliness, be one of the reasons we don't factor Christ's character into the story of Judas? Are we so personally offended by what happened to our beloved Savior, that we take pleasure in concluding—*No mercy for Judas?*

If Judas had betrayed one of the other disciples instead of Jesus, wouldn't we balance Judas' actions against an abundance of Scripture before deciding about his fate? Are we so emotional over what Judas did to Jesus that we delight in considering his soul a write-off? Conversely, if we conclude that Jesus did extend mercy to Judas, despite the betrayal, we'd have no excuse for denying mercy to others, especially for offenses that pale in comparison. When we refuse to extend mercy to someone, we deprive that person and any observers of what should have been an inspiring lesson imparted through our faithful witness.

Since Jesus is our pattern for living, imagine how our perspective would change with the knowledge that Jesus showed mercy to Judas. It would allow us to see Judas' self-inflicted death on the tree as revealing the depth of God's *mercy* toward humanity, in the same manner that Jesus' death on the tree reveals the depth of God's *love* for humanity. By denying mercy to Judas, the only one who gets any glory is our adversary.

Just think of the potential damage to Satan's kingdom if every believer understood the depth of God's love and mercy and applied those principles toward blessing others. It would allow the "Fruit of the Spirit" to manifest within us, as to leave little place for selfishness or any other work of the flesh (Galatians 5:19-24). Satan works relentlessly through any pain and selfishness to ensure that Christ's well-intentioned followers feel justified in withholding mercy whenever they think it's undeserved.

> *Mercy for Judas* promotes a mindset that will change the way believers view and interact with all people

Some commentators assert that Judas' heart was not right before God because when he approached Jesus with the soldiers (Mark 14:45), he referred to Him by the lesser title of "Rabbi" instead of "Lord." Though this reads something into the text, it could perhaps reflect Judas' waning attitude after hearing that Jesus would be crucified. As the Passover supper neared and Jesus spoke increasingly of His impending death, Satan imposed upon Judas' declining attitude and snared his heart:

*"And supper being ended, **the devil having already put it into the heart of Judas Iscariot**, Simon's son to betray Him..."*

(John 13:2)

Matthew's gospel tells us that on the evening of the betrayal, Jesus sat down with the Twelve Apostles and said:

*"Assuredly, I say to you, one of you will betray Me." And they were exceedingly sorrowful, and **each of them began to say to Him, 'Lord, is it I?'** He answered and said, 'He who dipped his hand*

*with Me in the dish will betray Me. The Son of Man indeed goes just as it is written of Him, **but woe to that man by whom the Son of man is betrayed! It would have been good for that man if he had not been born.'** Then Judas, who was betraying Him, answered and said, **'Rabbi, is it I?'** He said to him, 'You have said it.'"*

(Matthew 26:21-25)

Many commentators use the above passage as proof that Judas' soul is forever lost, but they base that on what? Stealing money? Deception? Betrayal? These infractions alone, if anything, might possibly lead to one's physical death, but spiritual death entails a different criterion. We'll discuss that later.

Many of us know all too well the pain of theft, betrayal, deception, and slander. If a person sins against us in one of these areas and later publicly confesses it, and declares us innocent of any wrongdoing, wouldn't God require us to show mercy to that person? Showing mercy is having compassion; and because Jesus is most merciful, wouldn't it be uncharacteristic of Him to walk with Judas for 3 years, fully aware of his inevitable sin, and yet allow Judas to go to his death without endeavoring to preserve his precious soul?

Note the difference in how Jesus dealt with Peter after warning him of being targeted by Satan.

"And the Lord said, 'Simon, Simon! Indeed, Satan has asked for you, that he may sift you as wheat. **But I have prayed for you,** *that your faith should not fail; and when you have* **returned to Me,** *strengthen your brethren.'"*

(Luke 22:31-32)

This warning came after Jesus declared that whoever denied Him, He would also deny.

"Therefore whoever confesses Me before men, him I will also confess before My Father who is in heaven. **But whoever denies Me before men, him I will also deny before My Father who is in heaven."**

(Matthew 10:32-33)

As predicted, Satan's sifting of Peter resulted in Peter's denial of Christ, which apparently Jesus could observe from His location.

"And a certain servant girl, seeing him as he sat by the fire, looked intently at him and said, 'this man was also with Him.'" **But he denied Him,** *saying, 'Woman, I do not know Him.'" ...Then after about an hour had passed, another confidently affirmed, saying, 'surely this fellow also was with Him, for he is a Galilean,'" But Peter said, 'Man, I do not know what you are saying!' Immediately, while he was still speaking, the rooster crowed. And* **the Lord turned and looked at Peter."**
(Luke 22:60)

"Then he began to curse and swear, saying, 'I do not know the Man!'"
(Matthew 26:74)

After Jesus' resurrection, Peter's interactions with Jesus prove that Peter repented for denying the Lord (John

21:14-17). Obviously, Jesus extended mercy to Peter but what about *mercy for Judas?*

Did Jesus pray for Judas as He did for Peter?

We can understand why Jesus wouldn't have prayed for Judas to remain faithful *prior* to the betrayal; for being God in human form, His prayer would've resulted in Judas' faithfulness, thereby, thwarting the mission to the Cross. But what about *after* the betrayal? Wouldn't Jesus' unwillingness to pray for Judas' soul cause Jesus to appear unloving, uncaring, and unmerciful?

In Matthew 18:21-35 Jesus taught his disciples that **failing to grant forgiveness to a remorseful brother is sin.**

"So when his fellow servants saw what had been done, they were very grieved, and came and

38

told their master all that had been done. Then his master, after he had called him, said to him, 'You wicked servant! I forgave you all that debt because you begged me. Should you not also have had compassion on your fellow servant, just as I had pity on you?' And his master was angry, and delivered him to the torturers until he should pay all that was due to him. So My heavenly Father also will do to you if each of you, from his heart, does not forgive his brother his trespasses."

(Matthew 18:31-35)

> The very notion of no mercy for Judas seems to violate the compassionate praiseworthy character of the Messiah

Many commentators depict Judas as having undesirable or even evil character; yet much of it is guesswork. People in the first century weren't much different from people today: We begin good, things happen, we react stupidly, it becomes a disaster, we hope for mercy.

In John 13:18, Jesus quotes from Psalms 41:9, which gives us a sense of what He expected of Judas.

*"I do not speak concerning all of you. I know whom I have chosen; but **that the Scripture may be fulfilled,** 'He who eats bread with Me has lifted up his heel against Me.'"*

(John 13:18)

It's unclear as to whether Judas' betrayal was rooted in greed, a desire to expedite a new kingdom ruled by Christ, the hope of gaining favor with the Sanhedrin, a spiteful reaction to the shocking news of Christ's impending death, or the thought of having wasted three years of his life for nothing. However, what is clear from the above Scripture is that Jesus knew that Judas would betray Him. This flaw in Judas' character is the reason that he was chosen to be Christ's disciple. All of Jesus' followers have flaws; God's plan is to use all of us to His glory.

The following verses attest to the fact that Jesus knew the thoughts of men:

*"But Jesus, **knowing their thoughts,** said: 'Why do you think evil in your hearts?'"*

(Matthew 9:4)

*"But Jesus **knew their thoughts,** and said to them: 'Every kingdom divided against itself is brought to desolation....'"*

(Matthew 12:25)

*"But when Jesus **perceived their thoughts,** He answered and said to them, 'Why are you reasoning in your hearts?'"*

(Luke 5:22)

*"But **He knew their thoughts,** and said to the man who had the withered hand, 'Arise and stand here.'"*

(Luke 6:8)

*"And again, 'The LORD **knows the thoughts** of the wise, that they are futile.'"*

(I Corinthians 3:20)

*"O LORD, You have searched me and known me. You know my sitting down and my rising up; **You understand my thought afar off.** You comprehend my path and my lying down, And are acquainted with all my ways. For there is not a word on my tongue, but behold, O LORD, You know it altogether."*

(Psalms 139:1-4)

Furthermore, Judas committed and confessed his sin prior to Jesus' Crucifixion. Therefore, if mercy were extended to Judas, having received and believed the truth about Jesus, all of Judas' sins would've been carried to the Cross (John 17:3-8), (John 6-37-40).

"If we confess our sins, He is faithful and just to forgive us our sins and to cleanse us from all unrighteousness."

(I John 1:8-9)

After walking with Jesus for over three years and having first-hand knowledge of Christ's unfailing love, it's unrealistic to think that Judas would take his own life before uttering the words, *God, forgive me.* Certainly, Judas would've known that if he confessed his sin, returned the silver, and acknowledged the truth about Jesus, not even crucifixion could exhaust Christ's love and mercy toward him. Still, the guilt of betraying his Master was too much for Judas to bear.

So, how are we to understand the Lord's description of Judas as the *"lost son of perdition?"*

> *"While I was with them in the world, I kept them in Your name. Those whom You gave Me I have kept; and none of them is lost except the son of perdition, that the Scripture might be fulfilled."*
> *(John 17:12)*

At this point it becomes necessary for a more theological treatment of this issue. Other than John 17:12, the phrase *son of perdition* appears only in 2 Thessalonians 2:3, where it indisputably describes anti-Christ, whom we know is destined for spiritual destruction. Many, therefore, insist that the doom, which is implicated by this phrase, must apply equally to Judas. This is, perhaps, what British biblical scholar James Barr[3] refers to as *illegitimate totality transfer;* the erroneous notion that a word in a particular context means the sum total of all (or even some) of its possible meanings.[4] It occurs when separate elements of thought are combined into a whole, not according to the usage of the author or according to the context. There's no evidence that Judas had anything in common with an anti-Christ or that hell was the context of Jesus' prayer.

The word "perdition," (apoleia, in Greek), which means *lost* or *damnation,* could apply to either one's spiritual or physical demise. At first glance, the idea of Judas' spiritual death, which is popular among commentators, appears difficult to refute. Yet in contemplating the flawlessness of Christ's character, the depth of His love and mercy, and by understanding the context of Christ's prayer in John 17:12, the term *(apoleia)* seems to refer more reasonably to *physical* death vs. spiritual death.

Additionally, when considered in its context and

in conjunction with Christ's character, the word "lost" (*apollumi*) appears more likely to refer to Judas losing his place among the Twelve Apostles and the privilege of advancing Christ's kingdom here on earth, than being damned to hell. Again, it's only by examining the context of the text and Jesus' character, and reflecting on the love and compassion that God has shown to others and to us, that mercy for Judas surfaces as the preferable outcome.

> It's God's mercy toward sinners that inspires violent-natured people to extend mercy to one another

Just as Jesus knew He'd be betrayed by Judas, He knew also that Satan would weaponize Judas' guilt and use it for the destruction of his flesh. And because Satan has no power at all against the enduring love and mercy of Christ, it's more reasonable to conclude that Jesus didn't despise Judas' broken and contrite heart, but rather, He delighted in preserving Judas' soul?

"The sacrifices of God are a broken spirit, A broken and a contrite heart---these, O God, You will not despise."

(Psalms 51:17)

"The LORD is with those who have a broken heart, And saves such as have a contrite spirit."

(Psalms 34:18)

Not without overwhelming proof should we embrace any belief that impinges upon the character and ways of our Lord Jesus Christ.

Jesus came into the world to save sinners *(I Timothy 1:15)*. The popularly held position regarding Judas' fate requires us to believe that before Jesus provided eternal life for even one soul, He willingly superintended the eternal destruction of His wayward apostle's soul. Does this sound like a divine plan?

"For the Son of Man did not come to destroy men's lives but to save them."

(Luke 9:56)

*God always acts in accordance with
His revealed character*

If we accept the traditional belief about Judas' life and fate without searching out the intended meaning and context of the applicable text, and without mingling those findings with our own inclinations, we miss out on vital lessons provided in Judas' story. These lessons serve as incentives for today's disciples to show Christ's love and mercy to a morally decaying world. We must be mindful of how easily Bible messages can be misconstrued if not viewed through the lens of Christ's merciful character and loving attributes.

As was mentioned earlier, failure to show mercy betrays our Christian character. In Luke 11:2, Jesus instructs His disciples to pray:

"Give us this day our daily bread."

This *bread* may include more than just food to sustain our physical body, but also, whatever resources we need (wisdom, finances, patience, longsuffering, self-control, etc.) that would enable us to please God. Jesus' *food* was to do the will of His Father.

"In the meantime His disciples urged Him, saying, 'Rabbi, eat.' But He said to them, 'I have food to eat of which you do not know.' Therefore the disciples said to one another, 'Has anyone brought Him anything to eat?' Jesus said to them, 'My food is to do the will of Him who sent Me, and to finish His work.'"

(John 4:31)

God's will for us all is that we manifest godly character, daily. This includes loving God and neighbor and showing mercy to others. When we betray our godly character by failing to be merciful, we're not much different than Judas. Betrayal is betrayal. And just like Judas, many who have an inclination toward betrayal do well until something threatens to interrupt their livelihood or their life's rhythm.

Imagine if the Lord showed Himself at our Christian gatherings and stated, *"There are some here who will betray My character."* Wouldn't those who believe themselves to be the target of His words and those who strive diligently to walk uprightly, both respond with

49

"*Lord, is it I?*" Haven't we all been guilty of some manner of betrayal? Many of us aren't much different from Judas; therefore, it seems reasonable to assume that the same matchless love that extends mercy to us today, is the same love that would've moved Jesus to have mercy for remorseful Judas.

> "*Jesus Christ is the same yesterday, today, and forever.*"
>
> *(Hebrews 13:8)*

To insist that a one-time act of betrayal proves Judas to be wicked and deserving of hell exposes a kind of thinking that is punishment-oriented, violent-natured, or simply lacks understanding of God's purpose and character.

*All that Jesus did, including His interactions
with Judas were entirely God's providence*

Where's Judas Spending Eternity?

4

FOR MANY, THE MEANING OF THE WORDS "LOST" AND "PERDITION," FOUND IN JOHN 17:12, ARE MADE CLEAR ONLY AFTER CONSIDERING THE CHARACTER OF CHRIST. Biblical scholars will often differ in opinion over the meaning of a particular text. "Meaning" is *context dependent*.[5] And because almost every text appears in the middle of a larger text, it is necessary, in order to understand a passage, to try and see how it fits into the larger literary unit(s) in which it occurs.[6] A biblical word may not mean the same thing in every place it occurs. The reader must ask what the speaker or writer is trying to accomplish, and how does this term serve those purposes?[7]

The Greek word for "lost" (apollumi), used twice in the parable of the prodigal son (Luke 15:11-32), is the same word used by Jesus in John 17:12 when speaking of Judas being lost. This word has several meanings, depending on the context:

1) to cause or experience destruction; ruin; destroy
2) perish, be ruined
3) **to fail to obtain what one expects or anticipates, lose out on, lose**
4) **to lose something that one already has or be separated from a normal connection, lose, be lost.**[8]

The use of the word "lost" *(apollumi)* in John 17:12 seems to align more fittingly with the above definitions 3 or 4, where the loss points to something *physical*.

"Those whom You gave Me I have kept; and none of them is lost except the son of perdition, that the Scripture might be fulfilled."

Within hours of Jesus speaking the above words, Judas would physically hang himself on a tree. Those who insist that this word "lost" refers to spiritual death, should make certain that they're not taking it out of context.

> *If you alter the context of a word or sentence, you alter the content of that text[11]*

Many biblical scholars hold to definitions 1 or 2, which accords with the traditional view that Judas was forever *spiritually* lost. This view equates the word "lost" *(apollumi)* with the phrase "son of perdition" found in 2 Thessalonians 2:3. Again, in that instance, the word "perdition" *(apoleias)* refers, undeniably, to the "man of sin" who is to experience spiritual destruction. The word *apollumi* denotes a process of perishing, and *apoleia,* the destruction that results.[9]

"Let no one deceive you by any means: for that

Day will not come unless the falling away comes first, and the man of sin is revealed, the son of **perdition,** *who opposes and exalts himself above all that is called God or that is worshiped, so that he sits as God in the temple of God, showing himself that he is God."*

(2 Thessalonians 2:3)

The Greek word for "perdition" *(apoleias)* also means: the destruction or ruin that one experiences. This ruin or destruction can be either [material], as in Matthew 26:8 regarding the **waste** of costly oil; or [physical], as in Acts 25:16 regarding Paul being sentenced to **die/destruction;** or [spiritual], as shown above in 2 Thessalonians 2:3 regarding the son of **perdition.**

Again, this Greek word *(apoleias)* used below means *destruction* and in this instance refers, unquestionably, to *physical* death:

*"... 'It is not the custom of the Romans to deliver any man to **destruction** before the accused meets the accusers face to face, and, has opportunity*

to answer for himself concerning the charges against him.'"

(Acts 25:16)

That the above refers to *physical* death is clear for it would be impossible for a Roman magistrate or any other human-being to deliver another human-being to *spiritual* death. Only God can do that. The Greek word for "destruction" used in Acts 25:16 is the same Greek word used for "perdition" in John 17:12. Both seem to refer to *physical* death. If the reference in John 17:12 were referring to *spiritual* death, it would be out of context with Jesus' prayer, purpose, and God's providence.

> *Biblical exegesis is understanding the text in its contexts*

Jesus' crucifixion, death, and resurrection mark the height of His earthly ministry. All that Jesus did, including His interactions with Judas, were entirely

God's providence—His determined will being worked out all the way to the Cross and beyond. To maintain that there's *no mercy for Judas* is to assert that God had already *purposed* damnation for Judas, even before he became an apostle.

When Jesus quoted *Psalms 41:9,* in *John 13:18,* isn't it possible that, in addition to showing a parallel between King David's experience with Ahithophel and His own experience with Judas, that Jesus sought to affirm Judas as having been His *trusted friend?*

"Even my own familiar friend in whom I trusted,
Who ate my bread, Has lifted up his heel against me."

(Psalms 41:9)

Did Jesus purpose to send His *trusted friend* to hell after walking with him for 3 years? Is that what a true friend would do? And with Jesus being our pattern for living, might not such disregard for Judas' soul serve to skew one's understanding of *friendship, trust,* and love. Isn't it really CHRIST'S CHARACTER that's on display in the Judas narrative?

The message of *Mercy for Judas* is one of love, healing, and forgiveness. If Jesus prayed for forgiveness for those who were responsible for His crucifixion and the ones who carried it out (Luke 23:34), and granted foriveness to the criminal on the Cross next to Him (Luke 23:43), why would it be unthinkable for Jesus to forgive His wayward disciple? To have the knowledge that Judas received mercy from the Lord would give hope to numerous guilt-ridden souls that perhaps the weight of their own errors might be lifted. It would give countless victims of abuse and betrayal a reason to be hopeful that they may love and trust again. Worth noting is that the hardened criminal on the other side of Jesus, having no fear of God, did not benefit from Jesus' prayer for forgiveness.

Imagine the powerful positive impact on people of faith around the world if they believed that love and mercy were Jesus' only thoughts toward Judas? Such knowledge would strongly accentuate the message of I Corinthians 13:5, that "love thinks no evil."

> *Human mercy toward others is patterned after God's mercy toward sinners*

Betrayal is always ugly and unsettling, and in these days, an increasingly common occurrence. It's rare today to find a person who hasn't been its victim or the perpetrator. However, to insist that a one-time act of betrayal proves Judas to be wicked and deserving of hell exposes a kind of thinking that is punishment-oriented, violent-natured, or simply lacks understanding of God's purpose and character.

If we allow God's word and abundant love to rule our hearts, we'd shun the propensity toward punishment and violence. Also, we'd realize that Jesus didn't model a violent and retaliatory nature, but rather, a consistent exceptional capacity to love and forgive and a willingness to deliver all who seek restoration. If you distort Christ's character, you make the unshakable Rock on which the body of Christ stands, appear shaky in the eyes of the world, making it difficult for them to trust him.

> *To believe that there's no mercy for Judas creates a perpetual workplace for the devil*

After examining the Scriptures that pertain to Judas, it appears that betrayal was the only action taken by Judas that one might label as wickedness. And because we are unable to pinpoint, indisputably, Judas' motive for betrayal, we can't even say, emphatically, that his intent in that instance was wicked. "Wickedness" is defined as: *departure from the rules of the divine or the moral law; evil disposition or practices.*[10] Other than betraying Jesus and stealing insignificant amounts of money, there's no clear evidence to conclude that Judas ever embodied wickedness or was deserving of damnation.

Hell is traditionally believed to be the place of eternal absence of God, a place to be occupied exclusively by those who have renounced God and have embodied or practiced wickedness. So, where will Judas spend eternity? This author contends that hell was never God's plan for Judas nor Judas' will for himself. The hope, therefore, is that Judas will share the same fate as those who believe and treasure God's word in their heart—cherished and nestled in an expectation of mercy.

The mercy we extend to others is rooted in our understanding of God's gracious out-pouring of mercy on sinners. Therefore, it's important that we contemplate the aftermath of Judas' betrayal

Where violence is unrecognized as violence,
it becomes acceptable

Fruit of the Fall

5

AS CULTURES MOVE FURTHER AWAY FROM GOD, VIOLENCE INCREASES AROUND THE WORLD. At the root of most unjust acts of violence is selfishness. Violence is often used to advance one's personal interests or happiness, without regard for the interest, happiness or well-being of others. However, it didn't start out that way. The sinful act that caused the first couple to fall from innocence is what introduced violence (the fruit of the fall) into the world.

Human history began in Genesis 1:31 where God expressed His pleasure with all that He created on the earth. God made the first man, Adam, and placed him in the Garden of Eden to live, tend and keep it.

"And out of the ground the LORD God made every tree grow that is pleasant to the sight and good for food. The tree of life was also in the midst of the garden and the tree of the knowledge of good and evil."

(Genesis 2:9)

God gave clear command to Adam regarding the sacred tree:

"And the LORD God commanded the man, saying, of every tree of the garden you may freely eat; but of the tree of the knowledge of good and evil you shall not eat, for in the day that you eat of it you shall surely die."

(Genesis 2: 16-17)

God then made Eve as a companion for Adam, and she was subjected to the same commands as given to him. The third chapter of Genesis reveals how the serpent cleverly deceived Eve into violating God's command:

> *"Now the serpent was more cunning than any beast of the field which the Lord God had made. And he said to the woman, 'Has God indeed said', 'You shall not eat of every tree of the garden?'"*
> *"And the woman said to the serpent, 'We may eat of the fruit of the trees of the garden; but of the fruit of the tree which is in the midst of the garden, God has said, 'You shall not eat it, nor shall you touch it, lest you die.'"*
>
> *(Genesis 3: 1-3)*

Adam and Eve were provided with everything they'd need for sustenance and pleasure. Yet the serpent, by deceptively twisting God's Word, instigated Eve to snatch fruit from the one tree that God reserved for Himself (Genesis 3:4-5). *The unauthorized taking of what belongs to another, against his or her will, is an act of violence.* This author's definition of violence includes also: *the selfish trampling of another's will or any act that intentionally ruptures the alignment of human will and the will of God.* That's precisely what occurred with the first couple.

Therefore, the sin that caused their fall was triggered by violence and the subsequent *curse* perpetuated a cycle of violence, until the earth was filled with it.

"Then the LORD saw that the wickedness of man was great in the earth, and that every intent of the thoughts of his heart was only evil continually."
(Genesis 6:5)

The earth also was corrupt before God, and the earth was filled with violence. So, God looked upon the earth, and indeed it was corrupt; for all flesh had corrupted their way upon the earth. And God said to Noah, 'The end of all flesh has come before Me, for the earth is filled with violence through them; and behold, I will destroy them with the earth.'"
(Genesis 6:11-13)

Although acts of violence may not always include physical harm, there's hurt that's felt in nearly every occurrence. Violence is so ingrained in our society today that it's considered naïve to expect mercy or fairness from anyone. And the idea of extending mercy to adversaries is disparaged by many as foolishness.

This is one reason that so many people have difficulty embracing and interpreting God's Word, because their worldview and outlook on life are largely and inextricably shaped by violence. If we understand that God's thoughts and ways are higher than our thoughts and ways (Isaiah 55:8-9), then we should also accept that God's mercy goes much further than we might imagine.

The definitions of violence mentioned earlier are captured in the story of David and Bathsheba. It's indisputable that King David's ordering of the death of Uriah, solely to cover-up the king's sin with Bathsheba, was an egregious act of violence (II Samuel 11:14-17). Yet many would be unwilling to characterize the act of taking Bathsheba in adultery as violence. Where violence is unrecognized as violence, it becomes acceptable.

Nothing better reveals our propensity for violence than a threat against the happiness or well-being of our loved ones. In such instances, unless we allow a

Could it be that mercy is a matter much weightier than the Church has historically recognized?

full release of the Holy Spirit within our being, that deep-seated violence will surface without any regard for mercy. An example of this is found in Luke 22:49-53, where the apostle Peter felt the need to protect Jesus from the violent-hearted multitude who sought Him with clubs and swords. Peter, without mercy and without considering the Lord's will, drew his sword and cut off the ear of the high priest's servant. Jesus had mercy on the man and healed his ear.

> *The potential for violence increases whenever we fail to consider God's will before we act*

Just prior to the above incident with Peter, Jesus had given His disciples a new commandment to love one another as He had loved them (John 13:34). The hour had come for Jesus to inaugurate a New Covenant, which would be characterized by a *nonviolent way of living marked by mercy.* The Old Covenant was rooted in sacrifice and required natural material sacrifices when worshipping God. Israel would offer sacrifices as an expression of worship, dependence, and obedience to Yahweh. However, the New Covenant would represent a radical change that calls for *spiritual* sacrifices:

> *"...you also, as living stones, are being built up a spiritual house, a holy priesthood, to offer up spiritual sacrifices acceptable to God through Jesus Christ.*
>
> *(I Peter 2:5)*

New Testament worshippers are called to be imitators of God:

> *"Therefore be imitators of God as dear children. And walk in love, as Christ also has loved us and given Himself for us, an offering and a sacrifice to God for a sweet-smelling aroma."*
>
> *(Ephesians 5:1-2)*

This nonviolent way of mercy springs from the heart of God and flows through renewed minds, thereby, prompting a changed worldview. Extending mercy to others is one of the primary ways that we demonstrate love and commitment, in order to *"prove what is that good and acceptable and perfect will of God." (Romans 12:1-2)*

Again, holiness, mercy, and love are the height of God's character. Psalms 106:1 tells us that "His mercy endures forever" and "His love never fails" (I Corinthians 13:8). If these two qualities were actualized within us, it would significantly change the way we view, value, and treat other people, especially of our own family. The mercy that we extend to others is rooted in our understanding of God's gracious out-pouring of mercy on sinners. Therefore, it's vitally important that we contemplate the aftermath of Judas' betrayal.

> *Mercy for Judas, if true, would afford an unprecedented model of compassion and forgiveness*

There's much to learn from Judas' story but many believers aren't interested in studying about a seemingly lost soul. Since many theologian scholars have concluded that Judas is eternally doomed, the position held by most believers is that the scholar's conclusions must be true, no questions asked. On the other hand, if we accept as true that mercy was extended to Judas, it'll provide a treasure-trove of reasons for introspection and prompt all who put their trust in Christ to examine more closely their faith. If it were known that Jesus extended mercy to Judas, no biblical account would have greater capacity to reorient our thinking and inspire us to deal mercifully with others, than the story of Judas.

For too long our adversary has reveled in the glory of having prevailed over Judas' soul. But is that true? Satan is the "father of lies" and the master of deception. If believers truly understood Jesus' extraordinary character, the magnitude of His victory on the Cross, the immensity of Jesus' poured-out love, and the power of His resurrection, perhaps they'd recognize that Satan's victory over Judas was temporary, involving only Judas' body, not his soul. Such knowledge would reveal our adversary as the defeated foe that he is and diminish his capacity to instill fear into the hearts of believers.

At first glance Judas' role in the crucifixion narrative may appear to be less crucial than it was. Keep in mind, Judas was chosen by God because his character was perfectly suited to facilitate Christ's mission to Calvary's Cross. The Pharisees were so convinced of Judas' determination to betray Jesus, that they gladly paid Judas the blood money in advance. (Mark 14:10-11).

If it were true that Judas was discontented with Jesus, what better witness to authenticate Jesus' claim to be *"the Christ, the Son of the Blessed" (Mark 14:61-64)* than a disgruntled apostle. This truth about Jesus was proclaimed when Judas returned the money and declared that he had betrayed *"innocent blood" (Matthew 27:4)*. What a powerful confession! Although the Pharisees wholly rejected his declaration, Judas' closeness to Christ made him an undeniably credible witness. Ironically, the betrayer turned out to be the lone voice to speak in defense of Jesus, attesting that He was innocent of blasphemy.

Failure to appreciate Judas' vital role in God's plan of salvation has enabled a mindset among many that is eager to punish, particularly for offenses committed by people of little concern to them. Conversely, if mercy for Judas were affirmed in our hearts, it would cause us to be more loving, trusting of God, and merciful.

No doubt most people see themselves as being merciful and free of violence; they've likely never considered the extent to which anger and violence may have influenced their worldview. Knowledge of God's enduring mercy can radically change a heart, replacing the inclination toward revenge and punishment with a passion for uncovering truth. One's search for truth in regard to Judas' betrayal might reveal that sympathy, not contempt, is what Jesus felt as He dipped the bread and gave it to Judas (John 13:26-27). Perhaps, at that moment, Jesus reflected on His own encounter with Satan in the wilderness and the timeless lie used effectively by Satan throughout human history: Just do it! You'll feel better! Nothing can go wrong!

"Then the devil took Him up into the holy city, set

Him on the pinnacle of the temple, and said to Him, "If You are the son of God, throw Yourself down. For it is written: He shall give His angels charge over you, and, In their hands they shall bear you up, Lest you dash your foot against a stone."'

(Matthew 4:1-10)

Just do it! Jump down, Jesus! This is the same lie used on Eve in the Garden of Eden (Genesis 3:4). Take the fruit, Eve! Nothing can go wrong! It also worked effectively on Judas in the Garden of Gethsemane (Matthew 26:47-49). Satan convinced Judas that Jesus, the Messiah, who walks on water, raises the dead, and calms the raging sea, would never allow Himself to be overpowered and crucified. Therefore, just do it! Kiss Him, Judas! Nothing can go wrong!

*"For judgment is without mercy to the one
who has shown no mercy"*
(James 2:13)

6

THE SEARCH FOR TRUTH IS NEVER THOROUGH WHEN ACCOMPANIED BY THOUGHTS OF VIOLENCE. In Joshua 20:1-9, God knowing man's retaliatory instinct, instructed the children of Israel to establish six cities of refuge, places where a person who accidentally killed another could flee to escape the wrath of the murdered person's loved one (the avenger of blood). Within those city limits the fleeing person would be safe. If God took such care in the Old Testament to provide for the person who accidentally caused another's death, would He not have made some provision for Judas, who fulfilled the role to which he'd been called? It would be pointless and out of character for Jesus to banish Judas to hell.

Some argue that Judas' ill-fated outcome had nothing to do with Jesus, rather, Judas was judged, and his horrible fate sealed by his evil actions alone. However, Scripture reveals that the *authority to judge humankind* belongs to Jesus.

"And Jesus came and spoke to them, saying, 'All authority has been given to Me in heaven and on earth.'"

(Matthew 28:18)

"For as the Father raises the dead and gives life to them, even so the Son gives life to whom He will. ***For the Father judges no one, but has committed all judgment to the Son,*** *that all should honor the Son just as they honor the Father. He who does not honor the Son does not honor the Father who sent Him. Most assuredly, I say to you,* ***he who hears My word and believes in Him who sent Me has everlasting life, and shall not come into judgment, but has passed from death into life."***

(John 5:21-24)

"For we must all appear before **the judgment seat of Christ,** that each one may receive the things done in the body, according to what he has done, whether good or bad."

(II Corinthians 5:10)

"Him God raised up on the third day, and showed Him openly, not to all the people, but to witnesses chosen before by God, even to us who ate and drank with Him after He arose from the dead. And He commanded us to preach to the people, and to testify that it is He who was ordained by God to be **Judge of the living and the dead.** To Him all the prophets witness that, through His name, **whoever believes in Him will receive remission of sins.**"

(Acts 10:40-43)

"And there is no creature hidden from His sight, but all things are naked and open to the eyes of Him to whom we must give account."

(Hebrews 4:13)

> *"Mercy triumphs over judgment"*
> *(James 2:13)*

When we consider the pervasiveness of violence (the fruit of the fall), could it be that mercy is a matter much weightier than the Church has historically recognized, one that God intended all generations to ponder, exercise, and promote?

> *"Woe to you, scribes and pharisees, hypocrites! For you pay tithe of mint and anise and cumin, and have neglected the weightier matters of the law: justice and mercy and faith."*
>
> *(Matthew 23:23)*

The long-held belief that Judas is eternally doomed is unlikely to change unless pertinent Scriptures are viewed through the lens of Christ's loving enduring character. Character is *personal moral nature revealed in action;*[12] and here, it's a key for unlocking the truth about Judas' fate. The hindrance that's perhaps most difficult for some to overcome is found in Acts 1:15-20, where Luke recounts Peter's directive to his fellow disciples after Jesus' Ascension:

> *"And in those days Peter stood up in the midst of the disciples (altogether the number of names was about a hundred and twenty), and said, 'Men and brethren, **this Scripture had to be fulfilled, which the Holy Spirit spoke by the mouth of David concerning Judas**, who became a guide to those who arrested Jesus; for he was numbered with us and obtained a part in this ministry.'*
>
> *(Now this man purchased a field with the wages of iniquity; and falling headlong, he burst open in the middle and all his entrails gushed out. And it became known to all those dwelling in Jerusalem; so that field is called in their own language, Akel Dama, that is, Field of Blood.)*

For it is written in the Book of Psalms:
'Let his dwelling place be desolate, And let no one
live in it; and, Let another take his office.'"

Peter's claim demands a close reading of the text. Exegesis (the careful historical, literary, and theological analysis of a text)[13] is a process of asking questions of a text to determine what's really going on. Therefore, the chief question to be considered from the verses below is: Was the Holy Spirit speaking prophetically through the mouth of David and was it regarding the fate of Judas Iscariot or of someone else?

"Set a wicked man over him, And let an accuser
stand at his right hand.

When he is judged, let him be found guilty, And let
his prayer become sin.

*Let his days be few, **And let another take his***
office.

Let his children be fatherless, And his wife a

widow.

Let his children continually be vagabonds, and beg;

Let them seek their bread also from their desolate places.

Let the creditor seize all that he has, And let strangers plunder his labor.

Let there be none to extend mercy to him, Nor let there be any to favor his fatherless children. Let his posterity be cut off, And in the generation following let their name be blotted out.

Let the iniquity of his fathers be remembered before the Lord, And let not the sin of his mother be blotted out.

Let him be continually before the Lord, That he may cut off the memory of them from the earth;

Because he did not remember to show mercy, But persecuted the poor and needy man, That he might even slay the broken in heart."

(Psalms 109:6-16)

Both the above bolded words and the bolded words below are noted by Peter in Acts 1:20, as being the prophetic words of the Psalmist David concerning Judas' fate. Unpacking these words may help us answer the question of where Judas will spend eternity.

"Let their table become a snare before them, And their well-being a trap.

Let their eyes be darkened, so that they do not see; And make their loins shake continually.
Pour out Your indignation upon them, And let Your wrathful anger take hold of them.

Let their dwelling place be desolate; let no one live in their tents.

For they persecute the ones You have struck, and talk of the grief of those You have wounded.

Add iniquity to their iniquity, And let them not come into Your righteousness.

Let them be blotted out of the book of the living, and not be written with the righteous."
                                            (Psalms 69:22-28)

In both of the above passages, persecution of the helpless is what prompted those curses which cannot reasonably be linked to Judas. Character becomes key as we seek to know the truth of Peter's claims. Peter alone asserts that the **Holy Spirit spoke by the mouth of David concerning Judas.** There's nothing in these passages or elsewhere in Scripture that directly indicate that the Holy Spirit was speaking prophetically through David regarding Judas. Of course, opinions differ among scholars. Some scholars even question whether Psalm 69 was written by David or by Jeremiah (compare Jeremiah 15-15-18). We do know that parts of this psalm were applied typologically to Christ: *hated without cause (Ps. 69:4; cf. John 15:25),* zeal for God's house (Ps. 69:9; cf. John 2:17), *offered sour wine while on the Cross (Ps. 69:21; cf. Matt. 27:48).*[14]

Readers often presume upon traditionally held views of noted scholars. However, beyond the fact that all Scripture is given by inspiration of God (II Timothy 3:16), there's nothing to suggest that the Psalmist's words in Psalms 109 were anything more than his own passionate prayers. And if that's true, then we must ask ourselves: Are the words in question, spoken in Psalms 69 and 109:6-16, reflective of *divine guidance* or of *human feelings* aroused by the *fruit of the fall?*

> *"Let their dwelling place be desolate; let no one live in their tents."*
>
> *(Psalms 69:25)*

> *"And let another take his office."*
>
> *(Psalms 109:8)*

It's important to note that Psalms 69 isn't speaking to an individual but to a multitude. Verse 25 could apply to anybody and verse 26 doesn't relate to Judas at all. Additionally, in Psalms 109:6-16 the person that the psalmist is praying against had persecuted the poor and needy and slayed the broken hearted, and that, without mercy. This couldn't possibly refer to Judas. It speaks curses on his wife and children, and we have no indication that Judas had either wife or child.

The Bible was written in such a way that the aid of a commentary shouldn't be necessary in order to grasp its truths. Truth that cannot be determined by a close reading of the text in its context, looking through the lens of God's character and love, may have been taken out of context. Although portions of the Bible can be quite "deep," the Bible is not complicated.

Moreover, since Peter was the speaker in Acts 1:20, we must look closely at his character and his attitude at that time, to determine if he was truly speaking by the Holy Spirit. For we know that Peter wasn't speaking by the Spirit when he rebuked Jesus in Matthew 16:23. Could it be that seeing only eleven apostles instead of twelve became a nagging reminder to Peter of having denied knowing his Savior? Could unsettled emotions and feelings have incited Peter to see Psalms 69:25 and Psalms 109:8 as referring to Judas? Or could the belief that twelve apostles were needed to coincide with the twelve tribes of Israel have moved Peter to pursue, what possibly might have been, an impulsive and unauthorized choosing of a replacement for Judas? Opinions differ on this, so let's consider what we know to be true.

We know that the twelve original apostles were all *chosen* by God. The only time that the practice of *drawing lots* was used to choose a leader, was by Peter, here in Acts 1:26. Roman soldiers casting lots to determine who will get Jesus' clothing (Matthew 27: 35) can't begin to compare with trying to fill a divinely instituted office. And the move to replace Judas occurred perhaps a few days or hours prior to the out-pouring of the promised Holy Spirit, which Jesus told the apostles to go to Jerusalem and *wait* for (Luke 24:49). This action on the part of Peter seems more like getting ahead of God than being led by God.

"However, when He, the Spirit of truth has come, ***He will guide you into all truth;*** *for He will not speak of His own authority, but whatever He hears He will speak; and* ***He will tell you things to come."***

(John 16:13)

In the Old Covenant, Israel and her chosen leaders, prophets, and priest, were duly *called out* and summoned by God to serve Him faithfully.[15] In the New Testament, the spiritual "calling" of the servants and people of Yahweh was also initiated by the spirit of God. Paul uses the word "called," meaning God's effective call.

*"Through Him we have received grace and apostleship for obedience to the faith among all nations for His name, among whom you also are the **called of Jesus Christ;** To all who are in Rome, beloved of God, **called to be saints...."***

(Romans 1:5-7)

*"Paul, a bondservant of Jesus Christ, **called to be an apostle,** separated to the gospel of God which He promised before through His prophets in the Holy Scriptures...."*

(Romans 1:1)

For Christ Jesus, the Mediator of a new and better

covenant (Hebrews 8:6), to authorize the replacement of an apostle using the practice of *drawing lots,* would be out-of-sync with God's way, His mission and message. Even the choosing of deacons, in Acts 6:1-6, was a Spirit led decision through prayer and the laying of hands, *not the drawing of lots.* Still, some may say: But Peter was given the keys to the kingdom (Matthew 16:19). How is it that one can struggle with the idea of mercy for Judas but see nothing objectionable about Peter choosing an apostle by the *drawing of lots?*

Was the apostleship of Matthias God's initial will for replacing Judas (Acts 1:23-26)? Opinions differ. God has been known to place His blessing on certain relationships that were not His preference.

"Nevertheless the people refused to obey the voice of Samuel; and said, 'No, but we will have a king over us, that we also may be like all the nations, and that our king may judge us and go out before us and fight our battles.' And Samuel heard all the words of the people, and he repeated them in the hearing of the LORD. So the LORD said to Samuel,

'Heed their voice, and make them a king.'"
                              (I Samuel 8:19-22).

In Acts 1:16, Luke records Peter's declaration that *"the Holy Spirit spoke before by the mouth of David concerning Judas."* This asserts that Peter was led by the Holy Spirit to speak those words; but as previously stated, there's no clear evidence that Judas was prophetically the subject of Psalms 69 or 109. Do we dare question what has been written about Peter?

Exegesis is all about asking questions of the text and being free to hear its answers. The fact that Peter attributes the wrathful words of Psalms 69 and 109 to Judas is telling. Therefore, before accepting Peter's claims about Judas' fate, we must draw insight from all that Scripture reveals about the facts surrounding those claims, including Peter's character and state of mind at that time.

Slightly noteworthy is Peter's prayer in Acts 1:24-25, spoken shortly after Judas' death, before a group of a hundred and twenty followers; some of whom may have been close to Judas.

> *"You, O Lord, who know the hearts of all, show which of these two You have chosen to take part in this ministry and apostleship from which **Judas by transgression fell, that he might go to his own place.**"*

Regardless of whether the words "his own place" refer to *spiritual* or *physical* death, used at that time, they seem to be without sympathy.

Again, the question is, was Peter being *led* by God to replace Judas? Close reading of verse 18, which may or may not be Peter's words, sound more like the *fruit of the fall* than *the fruit of the Spirit.*

> *"(Now this man purchased a field with the wages of iniquity; and falling headlong, he burst open in the middle and all his entrails gushed out.)"*

No clear conclusions can be drawn from the above; however, a review of Peter's character, as displayed in other passages of Scripture, reveal a hasty, impatient servant who on occasions proved deficient in consistency and spiritual discernment.[16] Furthermore, we should consider the following examples wherein significant lessons about Peter's character can be drawn. Matthew 16:21-22, 15:15-20; Mark 9:2-6, 10:28-30, 14:27-31; Luke 5:4-8; Galatians 2:11-16. In seeking to understand where Judas spends eternity, we must factor into Judas' story the impulsive character of Peter and his past actions. It then becomes easier to see how Peter's emotions and feelings at that time, could've caused him to view Psalms 69:25 and 109:8 as being prophetic of Judas.

In Acts 15:36-41, Paul and Barnabas, two of the New Testament's strongest leaders, who travelled together ministering in many cities, parted company in sharp contention over the shortcomings of John Mark. This, because Mark failed to keep his commitment to the work. Was Paul being *led* of the Spirit to reject John Mark, refusing to overlook his missteps? Opinions differ. A close reading of the text may suggest that Paul's emotions and feelings at that time could've caused him to misstep, by failing to model the mercy, humility, love, and peace which, according to his teaching, is what God's followers are called to display.

> *"Therefore, as the elect of God, holy and beloved, put on tender mercies, kindness, humility, meekness, longsuffering, bearing with one another, and forgiving one another, if anyone has a complaint against another; even as Christ forgave you, so you also must do. But above all these things put on love, which is the bond of perfection."*
>
> *(Colossians 3:12-15)*

Toward the end of Paul's ministry, he instructed faithful Timothy to *"Get Mark and bring him with you, for he is useful to me for ministry." (II Timothy 4:11)*

Opinions differ as to who was right regarding the contention between Barnabas and Paul. The effectiveness of both of their ministries proves that *"All things work together for good to those who love God, to those who are the called according to His purpose"* (Romans 8:28). As with Paul and John Mark, we've all experienced regrettable missteps. Regardless of how earnestly we strive to advance God's kingdom, most of us will error in some way, even daily. Who among us haven't misused Scripture unwittingly? God delights to turn our errors into teaching opportunities. If Peter's words in Acts 1:16-20 turn out to be presumptuous, might it be that God intended, through Peter's misstep, to teach a valuable lesson about rightly dividing and meditating on Scripture? (II Timothy 2:15)

If Judas hadn't committed suicide but returned to ask for forgiveness during the 40 days that Jesus presented Himself alive after His Resurrection (Acts 1:3), would Peter have dealt mercifully with Judas? Would Jesus? In Acts 7:60 when the stiff-necked, uncircumcised in heart and ears witnesses were stoning Stephen, he cried out with a loud voice, *"Lord, do not charge them with this sin."* Compare Stephen's words with the words of Jesus spoken from the Cross: *"Father, forgive them, for they do not know what they do" (Luke 23:34).* If Stephen's last words to God were a plea for mercy for the men who were killing him, wouldn't Jesus—the personification of mercy, exemplify no less concern for His betrayer?

Again, God always acts in accordance with His revealed character. Proper exegesis will never misrepresent the character of Christ.

Because we all have and will no doubt continue to manifest *fruit of the fall,* God seems to be admonishing humankind, through the Judas narrative, to be mindful of the ruinousness of sin and selfishness. Moreover, God's greater purpose seems to be that through the relationship of Jesus and Judas, the majesty of God's mercy unfolds and becomes instructive for believers in every generation. Opinions differ; but as Romans 14:5 states:

"Let each be fully convinced in his own mind."

*The search for truth is never thorough
when accompanied by thoughts of
violence*

Robert E. Colwell

Since mercy for others is what our Lord requires of us, it's unreasonable to think that Jesus wouldn't extend mercy to Judas

Conclusion

7

AS PREVIOUSLY STATED, MOST CONSCIENTIOUS PEOPLE ARE DISTURBED OR ANGERED BY WASTE, ESPECIALLY OF THINGS THEY DEEM TO BE VALUABLE. I remember the feeling that gripped me while watching Gloria Stuart play the elderly Rose Dawson Calvert character in the 1997 film Titanic. Her most moving scene occurred toward the end of the movie, which was set 84 years after surviving the disaster. Rose returned to the location where the Titanic went down and while leaning over the rail of the ship, dropped her rare, expensive, one-of-kind blue diamond necklace into the sea. The thought of such waste lingered in my mind for days.

The movie began with a younger Rose and her rich, sophisticated fiancé, Cal, celebrating the Titanic's maiden voyage. Unexpectedly, during the trip, Rose met and fell in love with another handsome passenger named Jack. As the story progressed, Cal placed his extremely rare diamond into his jacket pocket and, without thinking, placed the jacket on Rose when she became chilled. She was wearing the jacket when the ocean liner began to sink. Rose was eventually rescued while still wearing the jacket, but her lover, Jack, succumbed to the icy water.

Eighty-four years later, Rose, now 100 years old and the only living survivor of the disaster, returned to the same spot where the Titanic sank. While strolling along the deck of the ship, clenching the diamond in her hand, and reminiscing about the unforgettable moments spent with Jack in that very spot, Rose leaned over the rail and the gem slipped from her hand into the sea.

I remember thinking, "Wow, what a waste!"

Rose, however, was unfazed by what she'd done. The contentment on her face as she gazed upon the water proved that her memories of Jack were far more precious to her than the diamond. Rose understood that in that place where truth alone is cherished, all material interests and even one's own wellbeing must bow to genuine love.

Shallow conditional love is easily disturbed whenever its valuables are wasted. True love endures. Few things are more "diamond-like" than a spouse who delights and endeavors to live peaceably with a waste-prone mate, while trusting God that nothing good about their marriage will be lost. What makes married couples particularly valuable for the advancement of God's kingdom here on earth is that marriage provides that unique setting where God's love is most dramatically exhibited. Therefore, despite adverse feelings and barring any remarkably abusive circumstances, every opportunity should be exhausted to recover any valuables of the marriage that may have been lost or misplaced. Failing to forgive, once the Holy Spirit has urged you to do so, may prove to be an unnecessary and regrettable waste.

And because anyone of us, at any time, can get-it-wrong, we must constantly seek the Lord's guidance through prayer in order to maintain our meaningful God-given relationships. As noted in the introduction of this book, Judas got-it-wrong when he became indignant at the pouring out of costly fragrant oil on Jesus' feet. Jesus admonished him for viewing it incorrectly as waste. About four days later, in a similar incident, all the apostles got-it-wrong when costly oil was poured out on Jesus' head:

> *"And when Jesus was in Bethany at the house of Simon the leper a woman came to Him having an alabaster flask of very costly fragrant oil, and she poured it on His head as He sat at the table. But when His disciples saw it, they were indignant, saying, 'Why this waste? For this fragrant oil might have been sold for much and given to the poor.'"*
>
> *(Matthew 26:6-13)*

Paul got-it-wrong, as is recorded in Acts 26:9-11:

> *"Indeed, I myself thought I must do many things contrary to the name of Jesus of Nazareth. This I also did in Jerusalem, and many of the saints I*

shut up in prison, having received authority from the chief priest; and when they were put to death, I cast my vote against them. And I punished them often in every synagogue and compelled them to blaspheme; and being exceedingly enraged against them, I persecuted them even to foreign cities."

In the above instance, which occurred prior to Saul's conversion, Jesus spoke directly to Saul (later called Paul) from heaven and informed him that it was He, Jesus, whom Saul had been persecuting (Acts 26:15).

Though we all get-it-wrong at times, mercy is what we all hope to receive from those who were affected by our errors. And when we find ourselves ill-treated by others, our prayer should be for their heart to change, that they would seek our forgiveness and that we'd be free and delighted to forgive them. Since mercy for others is what our Lord requires of us, it's unreasonable to think that Jesus wouldn't extend mercy to Judas.

"Let the wicked forsake his way, and the

unrighteous man his thoughts; Let him return to the LORD, and He will have mercy on him; and to our God, for He will abundantly pardon. For My thoughts are not your thoughts, nor are your ways My ways," says the LORD.

"For as the heavens are higher than the earth, so are My ways higher than your ways, and My thoughts than your thoughts."

(Isaiah 55:7-9)

In Romans 14:5, Paul reminds us that different people occupy different mental locations:

"One person esteems one day above another; another esteems every day alike."

Obviously, this book's author favors Mercy for Judas. However, we must be respectful of the thoughts and opinions of others and be mindful, therefore, of what Paul goes on to exhort in the above verse:

"Let each be fully convinced in his own mind."

. . . God's greater purpose seems to be that through the relationship of Jesus and Judas, the majesty of God's mercy unfolds and becomes instructive for believers in every generation

Sources

1. Webster's New World Dictionary, Fourth Edition. 1999

2. Ibid.

3. Barr, James. *The Semantics of Biblical Language.* Oxford: Oxford University Press, 1961, p 218.

4. Gorman, Michael J *Elements of Biblical Exegesis.* Peabody: Hendrickson Publihsers, 1998, p 96.

5. Ibid., p. 69

6. Ibid., p. 98

7. Ibid., p. 97

8. Danker, Frederick William. *A Greek-English Lexicon of the New Testament and other Christian Literature.* Chicago: The University of Chicago Press, 2000

9. *Dictionary of the Latter New Testament & Its Developments.* Wrath. Downers Grove: InterVarsity Press, 1997

10. *Webster's Dictionary*, 1913 supplementary Section.

11 . Gorman, Michael J. *Elements of Biblical Exegesis.* Peabody: Hendrickson Publishers, 1998, p.66.

12 . Packer, J.I. *Knowing God.* Character. London, 1973

13 . Gorman, Michael J. Elements of Biblical Exegesis. Peabody: Hendrickson Publishers, 1998, p. 8.

14 . *Bible Knowledge Commentary, Old Testament.* Psalms 69:34-36. SP Publications, Inc. 1985

15 . Renn, Stephen D. Expository Dictionary of Bible Words. Called. Peabody: Hendrickson Publishers, 2005.

16 . Smith's Bible Dictionary. Peter. William Smith, 1884

About the Author

Robert E. Colwell was orphaned at age eleven and shuffled through different foster homes in New York. His high school principal, whose office Robert often visited, saw his potential, and urged Robert's English teacher to allow him to graduate. Robert's gratitude for God's outpouring of love and mercy despite his foolishness, made it easy for him to sympathize with the foolishness of Judas.

Robert is the Pastor of Calvary Chapel Crenshaw in Los Angeles, California. As an advocate for foster children and families with special needs, Robert has been a keynote speaker at state and national conferences in 28 states. He is a songwriter and playwright and has recently written a new musical with fourteen original songs. Robert earned a master's degree in theology from Fuller Theological Seminary. He and his wife Angela reside in Inglewood, California and have four adult children and two grandchildren.

Notes

Notes

Notes

Notes

Notes

Notes

Notes

Notes

Notes

Notes